The Modern Darling's Guide to Living City Chic on a Small-Town Budget

ISBN 1453690964

EAN-13 9781453690963

Printed in the United States of America.

MODERN

—adjective

Of or pertaining to present and recent times; not ancient or remote.

DARLING

—noun

A person or thing in great favor; a favorite of society or in social circles.

A modern darling is always lovely, kind and considerate. She is neither stuffy nor traditional. She is poised, carries herself with character, and remains calm and confident even in the most upsetting situations. Modern darlings are all ages and ethnicities, for being a modern darling is a state of mind!

Gratitude

Without you, this modern darling wouldn't be. I have to give you all the thanks and praise before this journey begins. To my Lord, I thank you for entrusting me, one girl, with a vision! Thank you to my mother, who has pushed me and molded me, even when I didn't know it, into the woman I now stand tall in. She is a queen, with grace, love and kindness like no other. And thank you to the darlings whose grace, movement, style and dignity have inspired me: CoCo Chanel, Lena Horne, Niki Giovanni, Simon Doonan, Bethann Hardison, Suzan-Lori Parks, Toni Morrison, Andre Leon Talley, and Cathy Hughes.

Thank you.

Table of Contents

Introduction

Fashion

Highs & Lows

The Foundation Upon Which Style is Built

Sweet Aroma

Beauty & Maintenance

Hair Tales

Fingers & Toes

Putting Your Best Face Forward

Make-up Wonders

Home

Interiors

Market Affairs

Entertaining

Correspondence

Out & About

Freebies

Theater

A Gal about Town

Travel 101

Current Events

Knowledge is Power

Pro Watch

Salutations

Shopping Guide

Recipes

Introduction

Let's be honest: every lady wants to live a fabulously chic lifestyle! We all want to be head-turning, trendsetting women with envious girlfriends—right? So let me ask you, what if you could live a fabulous life on a dime? And, what if it were possible to score the most current trends without breaking the bank? What if you were invited to attend the most exclusive events and were known to host the most exquisite social soirées? Well, darling ... you can!

City chic is a way of life. While I wish I could say it were effortless, the truth is, even the chic have to work at it! There's a quote by Yves Saint Laurent that I adore: *"Fashions fade, but style is eternal."* Translation: You can have every designer label in your closet and around your home, but if you don't know how to create your own signature style, those labels will begin to look like nothing more than cheap imitations. My motto is, "Only the stylish survive!"

The Modern Darling's Guide to Living City Chic on a Small-Town Budget is full of tips written to help you live a dashing life without a pricey tag attached. I hope you will enjoy your journey over the next few pages, and I hope that this is the beginning of you living fabulously city chic!

1

Fashion

Highs & Lows

Fashion and appearance are huge for every city chic darling. And every city chic darling lives by the rule of highs and lows.

The highs are all of your designer pieces—the must-have items that you would forfeit your rent money on! These are the items you wear because they are tailored, hang well on your body, and are made of the highest-quality fabrics. However, buying these items doesn't have to empty your wallet. You can hit up consignment shops, sample sales, and yearly blow-outs at retail stores to find all of your beloved designer labels at a fraction of the price that you would in boutiques.

The lows are the pieces that define your style and tell your story. They can be things you find in vintage stores and flea markets, your grandmother's diamonds and pearls, and the rare yard sale gem. You'll want to rack up on jewelry, accessories and the occasional dress, jacket, boots or skirt for all of your lows. Having the perfect lows is what makes your outfit an OUTFIT! But keep in mind that all of your Lows don't have to be found through scavenger hunts. You can find plenty of great pieces in trendy stores like H&M,

The Modern Darling's Guide to Living City Chic on a Small-Town Budget

---

Topshop and Zara, three retail chains that sell affordable runway-inspired styles.

The next essentials for the modern darling on a budget are her closet basics. These include the LBD (little black dress), crisp white shirts, several pairs of smart jeans, both black and neutral heels, a pair of jeweled sandals and a basic loafer. These can differ based on your style and body type, but you should still own all of them in some form. These are great items that will mix well with your highs, your lows, and your trendy pieces.

Last, but certainly not least ... always, always, always invest in great shoes & great bags. Nothing will make you feel more grown up and sophisticated than an expensive bag hanging from your shoulder, and a pair of pricey shoes on your feet.

Tip: Look to designers like Mary-Kate & Ashley Olsen for great examples of how to stylishly mix highs and lows. Even when dressed down, you can always count on these sisters to look city chic!

Foundation Upon Which Style Is Built

They say the foundation is the most important part of any building. It's the support of the structure it's holding. Well, my darling, this saying about the foundation is true for all things, including feeling city chic!

Your mother may have told you they should always match, and should never be worn and ratty, just in case of an unexpected trip to the ER. This is true, but they should also always match and never be ratty because daily they will be your foundation. I'm talking about your knickers! They're the closest things to your body throughout the day, and are thus the most important item through which you build the character of your tone. You know the feeling of wearing your best pair—you're more pulled together and confident. They can set the tone for your outfit, your mood and your outlook. You'll find yourself walking different—more astute and upright. You'll find yourself sitting and standing differently with more confidence and self-assurance, and from La Perla to Target you can find beautiful sets. A great one doesn't always have to cost three figures, but it can make the difference between being the city chic woman you dream to be, or the average take-'em-as-they-come-and-roll-with-the-punches woman you probably dread to turn into.

Tip: Whether bikini, thong or boy short, always go seamless to ensure a smooth and line free derriere.

Sweet Aroma

Every city chic darling has her own signature scent, and paying three figures no longer needs to apply. So say goodbye to expensive perfumes and say hello to essential oils. These yummy scents can be added to your pulse points (wrists, inside creases of your elbows, ankles, backs of your knees and thighs). And when applied to your hair, these little goodies are a twofold treat: they provide a day's worth of long-lasting aroma, and also give your hair a lively conditioning sheen. In stores like Lather, you can mix and match oils to create your own scents, or you can opt for oils that are already created and on the shelves. A couple of great ones are Carol's Daughters Tui Oil ($8.50) and Kiehls Original Musk Oil ($35). When choosing something that takes your fancy, just make sure you pick essential oils and not perfumed oils. The difference in the two is very important. Essential oils will add moisture when applied, while perfumed oils will take it away, as they are extremely drying to both the skin and hair.

Whether woodsy, sweet or floral, essential oils are a great way to find your signature scent.

Make people ask, "What's that you're wearing?" with the lingering notes of a scent created just for you!

2

Beauty & Maintenance

Hair Tales

While I would never recommend that you color or cut your own hair, I do suggest that you keep up with its daily and weekly maintenance at home. Why spend $65 on a shampoo, condition and blow-dry when you can purchase the same products your stylist uses and gain the same results yourself? Not to mention the time you'll save and the headache you'll avoid by not having to deal with all the gossip and cattiness that takes place in every hair salon. Sometimes all a darling wants is an exceptional and snappy shampoo and condition without any drama and over bookings!

When purchasing products for your at-home maintenance, you want to look for shampoos that have a nice moisturizing sud, rather than a bevy of bubbles. The difference between suds and bubbles is in the detergents used (something I learned while interviewing celebrity hairdresser Kim Kimble, who also has an amazing line called Kimble Hair Systems). The more bubbles (rather than suds), the harsher the ingredients—which means the harsher the treatment will be on your hair.

Doing it yourself is completely okay, but having the number of a great stylist on speed dial is still critical for any city chic darling. Investing in a created-just-for-you haircut is absolutely necessary. It'll make styling easier, you'll always look polished, and you'll be more inclined to do your hair every day versus throwing it up in a ponytail.

Fingers & Toes

There's nothing like the relaxed feeling you get after having a fresh mani and pedi. But even for this self-indulgent luxury, there are ways you can look polished while holding onto your dollars. You can start by getting a manicure and pedicure at the salon once a month versus once a week. And in between appointments, you can DIY with at-home treatments. Simply invest in a great sloughing cream, foot buffer, cuticle oil, nail and toe clippers, hand/foot lotion and a medley of nail colors. As long as you make sure you're buffing your heels nightly when you shower, and applying cuticle oil to your nails daily, you'll be good to go! Before going to bed, apply your foot cream and cover your feet with socks. This is for you single darlings only. If you're sharing your bed with someone, you can do this for an hour before heading to bed and again immediately after showering the next morning. No one wants to cuddle up with socks ... am I right? Besides, the chief results we want to achieve from our manis/pedis anyway are soft feet and hands, filed nails and flawless polish—and again, these results can be achieved on your time in the comfort of your home!

Tip: Schedule manis/pedis on the same day as your cut and color and make this your time for monthly overhauls.

Putting Your Best Face Forward

Skip the high-priced facials, and opt for ingredients from your kitchen. Things like honey, egg yolk, mayonnaise, avocado and oatmeal are highly beneficial to your complexion. Honey moisturizes, egg yolk tightens, mayonnaise conditions, avocado softens, and oatmeal exfoliates. Who would have ever thought that things from your fridge could be used to treat your skin? Well they can, and for no additional cost at all!

A city chic darling lives by her daily skin-care regime. One skin-care line that is absolutely amazing yet is easy on the wallet is Mario Badescu. With MB, you'll get luxury products without overpriced packaging (which, by the way, is what drives up the cost of many a beauty product). Oh, and did I mention, several of the Mario Badescu products have found their way onto the must-have lists of beauty mags like *InStyle* and *Vogue*? I guess it just goes to show that even the greatest "connoisseurs" of beauty will recognize a great product, no matter the tag, when they see one.

Eyebrow maintenance. This I wouldn't try at home, but it's also not a costly luxury to add to your routine. It seems so small, yet it's so incredibly big! Your eyebrows frame your face, and when maintained properly, they can be the difference between looking as if you just took a dip in the fountain of youth, or took a plunge into the depths of premature aging. Never, and I repeat never, have them plucked too thin. Clean only the unnecessary hairs along your brow line, leaving the majority of your brows still full. Also, invest in a brow pencil or shadow, so that just in case your esthetician makes a slip with the wax or tweezers, you can discreetly fill them in.

Tip: If you stay on top of these basics, you'll always look your best, even sans make-up.

Make-Up Wonders

Modern darlings should never go overboard when applying make-up. Remember, drama belongs to the night! Your make-up should enhance, and never cover up. Keeping your city chic look simple by lightly bronzing the cheeks, and applying a fruity tinted lipstick can go a long way. A bronzer that looks great on every complexion is Nars' in Laguna. Or you can really get the most out of your money and go with their Multiple Bronzer stick; it compliments every skin tone and can be used on the lips, eyes, cheeks and body. For the best in lip gloss that will outlast your day, try Stila's Lipglaze in Brown Sugar, Honeydew or Papaya. And if you prefer lipstick to gloss, opt for the Barney's exclusive, "Lipstick Queen."

One rule of thumb is to always go light on your lips if the drama is on your eyes. And vice versa: if you're going bright and bold on the pout, keep your eyes as neutral as can be.

Tip: Prime your lips with a concealer or a neutral-colored pencil. This will keep your gloss or lipstick in place, and will prevent losing color in the center of your lips. Also try dabbing a clear gloss in the center of the top and bottom of your lips for a more dramatic look. A great clear gloss with an unbelievable shine is Trucco's Divinyls Lip Gloss in Slick.

The Modern Darling's Guide to Living City Chic on a Small-Town Budget

★ In the back of the *Modern Darling's Guide to Living City Chic on a Small-Town Budget,* you can find tools to DIY kitchen ingredients, skin-care lines, mani & pedi products, and the best cosmetics, and eyebrow maintenance available.

3

Home
Interior

The home of a city chic darling should be her castle, but you shouldn't go broke trying to turn your apartment into a co-op. The bulk of the dollars you invest in your home should be spent on the basics (sofa, dining-room table, silverware, bed, linens and towels); everything else can be bought on a dime. Add some flavor and personality to your home by decorating it with inexpensive vintage items, flea market bargains, and family heirlooms. These thrifty finds, even down to your dining-room chairs, accent chairs, tables and dishes, will add a certain panache that you can't get from everyday retailers. A plus of not purchasing every item for your home in retail stores is that you will most likely come across some incredible one-of-a-kind pieces. And hunting for the perfect additions to spruce up your home can be a ton of fun when you score!

Another inexpensive idea for uplifting your home is painting. White walls are so ennuyé! Add a touch of color by painting accent walls in the main rooms of your home, or go all out and turn each room a different shade. Just be careful when selecting colors, and find tones that express your style, yet aren't blinding or massive eyesores!

Art is always a great option for adding flair to your home. It can get a bit pricey, though, so if you can't afford the Picasso you have your eyes set on, try arranging a mixture of mirrors and picture frames on a wall. Not only is it eye catching, it will add depth and character to any room.

Vintage finds mingled with high-end retail create amazing spaces full of character.

Tip: To personalize your room, frame old pictures of family, friends and objects of interest. Also shop flea markets and vintage stores for your frames.

There are a few items you can't skimp on, however, when living city chic. You'll always want to invest top dollar in your linen and towels. Listen, if you've never experienced sleeping on bedding with a 700 and above thread count, you don't know what you're missing. Who wants to lie on rough, beady sheets? Who wants to dry off with towels that are hard and leave residue after indulging in an incredible bubble bath? No one! Luxury linen and towels are an absolute must, must, must.

The Modern Darling's Guide to Living City Chic on a Small-Town Budget

Oh, and did you think that only you had to have a signature scent? Well, darling, your home needs one too! With so many yummy candles and diffusers to choose from, it can be quite overwhelming to select the right fragrance. When shopping for candles, go for soy-based ones. Not only will you be saving your walls from smut, you'll be saving the ozone, too! An added plus to soy-based candles is they tend to burn longer and a bit stronger, giving you more bang for your buck. And for those of you who are super eco friendly, why not try reed diffusers? My favorite (though I have to admit they're a bit of a splurge) are the Antica Farmacista diffusers in champagne (they are to die for).

Tip: Never go cheap on linen and towels; your skin will thank you for it!

★ In the back of the *Modern Darling's Guide to Living City Chic on a Small-Town Budget,* you can find Modern Darling's favorite luxury towels, linen and home scent lines.

Market

Food, food, food… the one area on which we all overspend and on which we are also the most wasteful. For starters, shop the farmers market instead of the supermarket; you'll save money on some items, plus all your produce will be very fresh! You can even catch great buys on fresh-squeezed juices, freshly baked breads, pastries and jams, and other knickknacks like candles and gourmet candy. For the items you do need to purchase from the grocery store, I'll let you in on a little secret: Wednesday mornings are the best times to shop. On Wednesdays, most stores are less crowded and the best deals hit the shelves. Most people tend to shop at either the beginning or the end of the week, and Wednesday is also the day that stores mark down items to make room for their end-of-the-week shipments.

Another money saver is buying less coffee—out, that is! Invest in a really great espresso machine. Sure, the up-front cost can be mind-blowing, but in the long run, think of all the money you'll save in just one month by not having to stop at your local café every day. An added bonus to this investment is the sophisticated look this machine will give your kitchen, and the charm you'll have by offering an espresso or cappuccino to your guests. How very grown up! And how very chic!

★ In the back of the *Modern Darling's Guide to Living City Chic on a Small-Town Budget*, you can find names of the best espresso, cappuccino and coffee makers available.

Entertaining

If you're anything like me, then you love entertaining in your home. And as a hostess, you want people to eat, drink and be merry—but you certainly don't want to run out of food or drink.

The menu sets the tone, and as a city chic darling, you want to make sure your guests are delighted with your spread. A simple hors d'oeuvre platter like vegetable crudités is a good choice—however, never, and I repeat never, buy the pre-made ones from your local grocer. Not only do they look wrong in every sort of way, the taste of pre-packaged and often dried-out veggies should never be apart of the menu of a city chic darling! Instead, opt for veggies like asparagus, eggplant, jicama, and Peruvian potatoes. And to spice it up a notch, blanch these veggies in a nice bouillon, or grill them in garlic and flavored olive oil. Not only will the colors pop, but the flavors will explode in the mouths of your guests!

Another easy tray to make is Multi-Seeded Crackers with a medley of Havarti cheese, Gruyere, goat, Brie and Mimolette. It's always a hit, and it's never dull and boring!

When it comes to drinks, everyone has a favorite, but this department is also where you can really rack up costs. One friend that saves me every time is Two-Buck Chuck! With a price tag of only $1.99 at Trader Joe's, a few bottles of Charles Shaw always come in handy. Don't be dismayed by the price of this award-winning wine, because it is fantastic! Charles Shaw has won a double gold medal in the Annual International Eastern Wine Competition, and has been voted Best of California and Best of Class for Chardonnays.

For the champagne enthusiast, the best month to purchase your favorite bottles is December. Because of the extreme competition among the champagne houses, prices are a lot lower during the holidays than they are at other times of the year. Stocking up at the end of the year will save you major bucks and time during the year to come.

However, if you're not into wine or champagne, another option is making signature drinks. A great way to do this and still ensure your cocktails will be a hit every time is to serve martinis and cosmopolitans. They're yummy, not too high in calories, and can be made in several different flavors. Not to mention, they look sublime when served! A martini I know you'll love is, you guessed it ... the Modern Darling!

Modern Darling Martini ™

(VeeV Açaí Spirits, limoncello, champagne and ice)

Fill a martini shaker with ice and add 1 shot of the chilled VeeV Açaí.

Add a tbsp. of limoncello and a splash of champagne. Cover the shaker and shake thoroughly.

Pour through a strainer into a martini glass. Stir once or twice, top with a thin swirl of lemon rind and one fresh mint leaf ... and enjoy!

Another fun supersaver is getting your guests involved. Try asking each person you invite to bring a bottle of their favorite wine or alcohol, while you provide the mixers, meal, ambiance and everything else. This way, 1) you won't have to worry about spending an obscene amount of money on drinks; 2) you won't run out of beverages; 3) you'll have a nice mixture of cocktails; and 4) everyone will have at least one drink they love!

★ In the back of the *Modern Darling's Guide to Living City Chic on a Small-Town Budget,* you can find recipes for a few quick yummy meals and hors' d'oeuvres.

Correspondence

With all the depersonalized convenience of texting, e-mails and e-vites, people hardly communicate anymore. Sometimes this electronic era is so déclassé. Show your friends, family, colleagues and loved ones how considerate you are by taking the time to handwrite your letters of thanks, and your "just wanted to say hello's." And what better way to show your sophistication and city chic style than by using monogrammed stationery? I know you may be thinking, "I thought this was a guide on how to live chic while saving money...." Well, darling, it is, and part of that is knowing when and where to skimp. E-mailing, e-vites and texting are perfectly fine for impromptu get togethers and gatherings. But for expressing to someone your thankfulness for a gift, or to invite someone to a soirée in your home, electronic communication can be downright tacky! While having your name flash across your loved one's Blackberry or iPhone is nice, think about how warm you can make them feel by hearing your voice, or by opening their mailbox and seeing a handwritten note you took the time to write, seal, stamp and mail.

Tip: If monogrammed stationery is too much of a splurge, go for a simple set and have a stamp in ink made of your name. Stamp each card, paper and envelope, and voilà: you have monogrammed stationery!

★ **In the back of the *Modern Darling's Guide to Living City Chic on a Small-Town Budget*, you can find a few of my favorite most affordable stationery and printing companies.**

Out & About

Freebies

Work the city in which you live, darling, don't let it work you!
There are always plenty of free events around—attend them. You
can hobnob with your city's finest even at functions with a $0 entry
fee. Did you know that the see-and-be-seen events never even cost
a dime to attend anyway? They may come with the price of
invitation only, but invitations aren't hard to come by for the
darling with impeccable social skills.

Find out what museums or art galleries are having free shows,
openings and exhibitions. Most cities also offer free concert series
in the park during the warmer months. Join an organization and
attend their monthly networking mixers; not only will you enjoy
complimentary drinks and hors d'oeuvres, you will also have the
opportunity to meet a few new faces along the way. And who
knows, these mixers may introduce you to the key people who can
get you into the invitation-only events. Broadening your social
circle is always a great thing, no matter what level in life you're on.
Remember, it's not always what you know, but WHO you know.

Theater

Visiting the empire state and want to see a Broadway musical? Wait till a few hours before the curtain rises to purchase your tickets. Some musicals have same-day sales that offer up orchestra seats at very inexpensive prices. But if you'd rather not take a chance on not getting a seat, get tickets for hit musicals for up to 50% off at the TKTS booth in New York's Time Square.

Travel 101

Want to get out of town? Wednesday to Wednesday is the best time to travel. The fare is almost always half the price of traveling on a Sunday or even a Monday. If you can't travel from a Wednesday to a Wednesday, at least booking your itinerary to depart or return on one will still save you extra bucks. And guess what day you'll most likely be able to upgrade or sit in a row that isn't full? Yep, a Wednesday!

A Girl About Town

With the price of gas today, who cares about owning a car (unless you live in a non-metropolitan area)? Besides, it's cheaper to arrive by cab, better by train, and best by walking—plus you'll get a great workout! Think *Sex in the City*—didn't Carrie and the girls always look so fabulously chic stepping out of their cabs with the wind blowing in their hair as they walked down the streets of New York City? You can too, darling!

The Modern Darling's Guide to Living City Chic on a Small-Town Budget

Tip: Spare your feet any pain and carry your heels in your purse, slide on a pair of flats, and hit the streets!

★ In the back of the *Modern Darling's Guide to Living City Chic on a Small-Town Budget*, I've listed the most comfortable and stylish shoes for walking.

5

Current Events

Knowledge is Power

A city chic darling is always in the know. Stay up to date on politics and current events in your city, and no matter where you live, read the NY Times. The NYT is a hub for all the news around the world. There's a reason this paper is called "the Grey Lady," with a tagline that reads, "All the News That's Fit to Print."

Reading newspapers on a daily basis is a great way to stay informed, and you'll become somewhat of a go-to gal—which is never a bad thing! Also, always have a classic literary work within your reach. You'll not only be able to contribute inspiring quotes and nuggets of wisdom to every conversation that takes place around you, you'll also look smart doing it! Remember, a darling who is well versed and well informed is a darling who will always reach the heights she has her eyes set on.

Pro Watch

Get inspired. Look to those city chic darlings you see walking your neighborhood, sitting next to you on the train, or gracing the cover of your favorite fashion magazine. While playing the copycat is never a form of flattery (it's really quite scary), someone else's style can inspire you to try something new. A book I love and that I completely recommend to darlings across the world is Simon Doonan's *Eccentric Glamour*. In this book he has single-handedly managed to collect eccentric beauties across many eras and completely break down their style. And when all else fails, look to the Modern Darling's blog for constant updates on the latest trends, style explosions and tips and tricks.

Tip: Other great reads include the *LA Times*, the *Wall Street Journal*, *Condé Nast Traveler*, *W*, and *Vogue*.

Salutations

So there you have it, my loves, tidbits on living city chic on a small-town budget. And as I'm sure you've picked up by now ... it consists of mixing highs and lows in almost everything you do!

Living on a budget isn't about completely cutting out the luxuries that bring you the most pleasure, nor is it about counting every cent. It's more a practice of shopping and indulging in moderation. Hey, even the wealthiest of the wealthy can enjoy the excitement of finding a great deal.

This is a book that everyone can learn something from, and it was very much written for me as well. I've been known to go a bit overboard at times, and I've had the not-so-pleasurable experience of having to pay the cards off from my shopping excursions too! I encourage you to share, share, share this book!

In closing, I wish you decades of happy shopping, one-of-a-kind vintage finds, flea market gems, magical freebie events and unforgettable soirées!

Shop smart, and remember to always stay city chic!

The Modern Darling's Guide to Living City Chic on a Small-Town Budget

Shopping
Guide

The Modern Darling's Guide to Living City Chic on a Small-Town Budget

Barney's New York Semi-Annual Warehouse Sale is worth the trip to NY or LA. You can get bargains of up to 50%–75% off on designer items. I'm talking Marc Jacob's and Manolo's for like 70 bucks! Barney's Warehouse Sale happens twice a year, typically in the last weeks of February and August.

Fred Segal/Ron Herman. During their twice-a-year clearance sale you can save up to 65% off all your designer items. And while you're there, if you've never been, do yourself a favor and visit their famed denim bar. You could walk away with a pair of 7 For All Mankind for $60, Citizens of Humanity for $70, or J-Brand and Goldsign for $70. Mark the months of January and September on your calendar to partake in this shopping extravaganza!

For the cutting-edge, trendsetting darlings, the Intermix twice yearly sample sale will save you up to 80% off retail price on brands like Stella McCartney, Chloé, and Matthew and Williamson.

For impromptu getaways with your guy, or for a girls' weekend away, look to timesaving sites like RentTheRunway.com. Starting at 10% off an item's retail price, you can rent designer frocks like Gryphon and Prabal Gurung for up to four days. Your rented item will show up to your home or hotel freshly dry cleaned in two sizes with a pre-paid envelope for its return. Can looking fabulous while saving cash be any easier?

Join Hautelook.com and BeyondTheRack.com, members-only online sample sales. Because these online events are exclusive, the sales generally last between 48-72 hours. So don't drag your feet on this one!

Find online store coupon codes at Dealio.com, and get the hottest daily deals from your favorite stores and designers. Simply log on to Dealio and type your favorite store into the search box, and a list of their current online coupon codes will be given to you. Get discounts of 30-50% off retail and some sale items, free shipping, and credits.

Swirl.com, presented by Daily Candy. Shop up to 70% off all designer brands, and save even more when you refer your friends. By sharing the love, you'll get a $25 credit for each friend you invite.

FASHION

Apparel

Renttherunway.com

Shoes

Tory Birch

Marc Jacobs Penny Loafer

Cole Haan

Beauty & Maintenance

Hair

Kim Kimble Products

Kera Care Products

Sally Hershberger

Manicures & Pedicures

Deborah Lippman Collection

Facials

Mario Badescu

Planet Green

Eyebrows

Anastasia

Damone Roberts

Make-up

Stila

Nars

Trucco

Lipstick Queen

HOME

Art Series

Igor & Andre

Luxury Towels & Bedding

Serena & Lilly

Candles & Diffusers

Antica Farmicista

Diptyque

Appliances

Delonghi Magnifica

Tassimo

Wine, Champagne & Spirits

VeeV Açaí Spirit

Charles Shaw

Correspondence

Papyrus

Polka Dots

Stampin

Newspapers/Mags

NY Times

LA Times

Wall Street Journal

Vogue

W

Conde Nast Traveler

Recipes

A few quick and yummy salads, hors d'oeuvres & the best desserts your guests will ever taste!

Salads

Tomato & Cucumber Salad

2 tomatoes cut into wedges. 1 cucumber, scored & sliced. 1/4 cup pitted ripe olives. 1/4 cup salad oil and 3 tbsp. lemon juice. 1/2 tsp. salt, 1/4 tsp. dry mustard and 1/8 tsp. garlic powder. Freshly ground pepper.

Directions:

In bowl, combine tomato wedges, sliced cucumber and olives. To make dressing: In screw-top jar, combine salad oil, lemon juice, salt, dry mustard, garlic powder and pepper. Cover and shake well to mix. Pour dressing over vegetables.

Cover and refrigerate several hours, spooning dressing over vegetables occasionally. Lift vegetables from dressing with slotted spoon. Can be served on top of leafy lettuce, if desired. Makes 4 servings.

Couscous Salad

8 ounces Israeli couscous. 2 tbsp. olive oil. 2 tsp. fresh garlic, minced. 4 ounces fresh spinach, julienne cut. 1/2 cup sun-dried tomatoes, diced. 1/2 cup black Calamata olives, diced.

1/4 cup red onion, diced. 1 tbsp. fresh oregano, chopped. 2 tbsp. fresh mint, chopped. 4 ounces feta cheese.

Lemon Vinaigrette. 1/4 cup lemon juice. 1/4 cup extra virgin olive oil. Sea salt to taste. Sugar to taste.

Directions: Cook the Israeli couscous according to package directions, then set aside and cool. Heat olive oil in a pot, then add garlic and heat for 30 seconds while stirring. Add fresh spinach and stir until wilted and fully coated. Set aside to chill. To make the vinaigrette, mix olive oil and lemon juice (whisk the mix). Add sugar and sea salt to taste. Add ingredients, excluding the feta cheese, and mix well. Chill salad. *Garnish with feta cheese right before serving.

Pasta Salad

2 cups thin Asian pasta. Cherry tomatoes, diced. Fresh garlic, chopped. 3 Tbs of Olive oil

Directions: Boil the noodles until soft, and set aside. Heat olive oil in a pan and sauté the fresh garlic until golden brown. Add the cherry tomatoes until the juices bleed. Take the garlic and cherry tomatoes and add into the pasta. Flip and rotate a few times to make sure all the ingredients are fully mixed.

*Serve with fresh orange roughy or any other meaty white fish.

Watermelon, Basil and Feta Salad

Cut up a watermelon and drizzle with olive oil. Sprinkle with crumbled feta and torn basil leaves. Season with sea salt and pepper to finish.

Hors d' oeureves

Hummus and Flat Bread

*This recipe calls for a food processor

One 15-ounce can of chickpeas (also known as garbanzo beans). One medium garlic clove, smashed and peeled. ¼ cup of Tahini. ¼ cup of Water. One medium lemon, cut in half. Pinch of salt. Extra-virgin olive oil. Ground cumin and paprika.

Directions:

Boil the chickpeas, then strain and rinse the beans under cool water. In a food processor, add the chickpeas, garlic clove, tahini, and water. Over the food processor, squeeze one lemon half into your hand, catching the seeds and letting the juice fall between your fingers. Save the other half of lemon for later. Add a touch of salt, a generous drizzle of olive oil, and any optional spices. Blend until smooth. After blending for a few minutes, check the consistency of the hummus. If it is not creamy enough, add water and continue to blend. Once it is thoroughly blended remove the hummus from the food processor and place in a serving bowl. Drizzle with little more olive oil the remaining lemon half, and serve with toasted flatbread.

For the flatbread. Thinly slice pita pockets or any other heritage grain bread. Place on a baking sheet, sprinkle with sea salt and bake at 375° for 7 minutes or until the bread is lightly browned and crispy.

Tapenade

2 cups pitted Nyon or Kalamata olives. 2 tablespoons capers. 2 anchovies (optional) . 1 clove garlic, crushed. 2 tablespoons olive oil. 1 tablespoon lemon juice. Pepper.

Place olives, capers, anchovies and crushed garlic in a food processor and blend until smooth. With the food processor on, pour in the olive oil in a steady stream to form a smooth paste. Stir in the lemon juice and season to taste with pepper. Place the tapenade in a jar and cover with a thin layer of olive oil. Serve with flat bread vegetables or seeded crackers.

Desserts

Fresh Mint Kisses

1/4 tsp. salt. 3 large egg whites. 2/3 cup sugar. 2 tsp. minced fresh mint

Directions:

Pre-heat oven to 375 degrees. Beat salt and egg whites with a mixer at high speed until foamy. Gradually add sugar, 1 tablespoon at a time, beating until stiff peaks form. Add mint; beat until blended.

Spoon mixture into a large zip-top plastic bag. Snip off a 1/2-inch opening in 1 bottom corner of the bag. Pipe 1-inch-round mounds onto parchment-lined baking sheets. Bake at 300° for 25 minutes or until dry. Cool on baking sheet 5 minutes. Remove from pan.

Lime Mango Sorbet

*This recipe calls for an ice cream maker.

1 cup turbinado sugar. 1 cup water. Zest from one lime. 1/2 cup lime juice. Touch of sea salt. 1 shot of VeeV Açaí Spirit.

Directions:

Heat the sugar, water, and lime zest in a medium saucepan until the sugar has completely dissolved. Set aside to cool. Cut the flesh from the mangoes, then chop the meat of the mango into chunks. In a blender, put the chunks of mango, sugar water, lime juice, and salt. Blend until completely smooth. Pour into a medium bowl, cover with plastic wrap, and refrigerate until completely chilled. When ready to put the chilled lime mango purée into your ice cream maker, mix in the VeeV Açaí Spirit. Blend the mixture in the ice cream maker according to its directions. After blending, transfer the sorbet into a plastic storage container and place in your freezer until firm. At least 6 hours. Enjoy!

Chocolate Pots de Creme

The charm of a petite pot de crème is in the presentation, because every guests will enjoy this treat from their very own little dish.

1cup half and half . 7 ounces dark chocolate, chopped. 3 tablespoons strong coffee (or decaf if you choose). 3 eggs. 2 tablespoons cognac

On low heat, bring the half and half to a light boil. Once boiling, remove from heat immediately and stir in the chocolate. Set aside for about one minute to melt, and then blend until smooth. Stir in the coffee and continue to mix. In a separate bowl beat eggs using a hand mixer until thick and frothy and then add them to the chocolate, making sure you mix well. Continuing to mix, you can now add in cognac.

After all the ingredients are mixed well and while they are still hot, pour the liquid into individual small dessert cups. Refrigerate for at least three hours. Serve cold and within.

These are just a few recipes I know your guests will love! But for more delicious Modern Darling's dishes, you'll have to purchase the upcoming book, *The Modern Darling's Guide to Playing the Perfect Host*, where you'll learn how to plan unforgettable soirée's, and host fabulous dinner parties, brunches and teas. It has all the rules to making sure your get togethers are the talk of the town!

NOTES

Be on the lookout for other titles from the Modern Darling's Guides, including:

The Modern Darling's Guide to Politicking

The Modern Darling's Guide to Playing the Perfect Host

The Modern Darling's Guide to Successfully Conquering the 1st, 2nd and 3rd Dates

The Modern Darling's Guide to Wooing your Boyfriend's Parents

Modern Darlings is a division of One Girl And A Vision, Inc.

OGAAV

Written by Gennifer McKissack

Edited by Claire Valgardson

Library of Congress Cataloging-in-Publication data is available on file.

www.ingramcontent.com/pod-product-compliance
Lightning Source LLC
Chambersburg PA
CBHW050829290526
45792CB00001B/314